BOOK 3 〉

PHONICS AND LIFE SKILLS READING
FOR
Adult Literacy, ABE, and ESL Students

Turning Learners into Proficient Readers

CONTENTS

PREFACE FOR INSTRUCTORS

Dear Instructors,

Equip your adult literacy and ESL students with the ultimate phonics resource that is designed to help them master the 44 sounds of English. This phonics and reading textbook offers a robust curriculum that includes reading activities, dictation exercises, writing, and vocabulary building.

This book's content is aligned with the English Language Proficiency Standards (ELPS) for Adult Education. It satisfies the expectations of the National Reporting System (NRS) and Workforce Innovation and Opportunity Act (WIOA), ensuring your ESL and ABE students are on the path to success.

Each lesson is carefully written to ensure students gain confidence and fluency by reading aloud, answering comprehension questions, and using vocabulary in context. With answer keys included, instructors can easily track progress and provide targeted support.

Starting with short vowel sounds and advancing through long vowel sounds, special vowel sounds, and various consonant sounds, this textbook provides a simple, comprehensive approach to phonics and reading comprehension. The structured lessons ensure that students consistently practice and reinforce their reading skills.

By practicing sounds and reading sentences and texts aloud, students will build a strong foundation in phonics, paving the way for improved reading skills. Indeed, this book is an essential tool that can help transform your classroom into a dynamic environment for phonics and reading mastery.

The CBL Team

INTRODUCTION FOR LEARNERS

Dear Students,

This phonics and reading textbook will help you master the 44 sounds of English and improve your reading comprehension skills. It presents engaging activities to build your reading, writing, speaking, and vocabulary skills. Each lesson will guide you through different sounds and provide practice opportunities to ensure you gain confidence and fluency in reading.

By reading aloud, answering comprehension questions, and using new vocabulary in context, you'll improve your reading and writing skills day by day.

In this textbook, you will find:

- Reading Activities and Strategies: Enhance your reading skills through diverse and interesting texts.
- Dictation Activities: Practice listening and writing skills by completing dictation exercises.
- Vocabulary Building: Expand your vocabulary with targeted exercises and contextual applications.
- Answer Keys: Check your progress and understand your mistakes.

The lessons cover essential topics, such as:

- Short Vowel Sounds: Starting with the basics to build a strong foundation.
- Long Vowel Sounds: Progressing to more complex sounds.
- Special Sounds: Understanding sounds like "ar," "er," and "or."
- Consonant Sounds: Mastering all the consonants in English.
- Special Consonant Sounds: Focusing on tricky sounds like "ch" and "sh."
- Vocabulary Exercises: Filling in blanks and reading sentences aloud to reinforce learning.
- Comprehension Questions: Reading texts aloud and answering questions to ensure understanding.
- Writing and Listening Exercises: Summarizing paragraphs and taking dictations.

This book will help you develop a strong understanding of English sounds, which will greatly improve your reading, writing, and speaking abilities.

Enjoy your learning journey!

The CBL Team

LESSON 1

SHORT VOWEL SOUNDS

Objectives:
1. Students will review and produce short vowel sounds.
2. Students will read short texts and answer comprehension questions correctly.

Exercise 1- Read and repeat the letters and sounds below.

Short Vowel	Examples
short a	cat, hat, bat
short e	pet, let, bed
short i	it, sit, hit
short o	top, hop, lot
short u	cup, pup, sun

Exercise 2- Read the following sentences aloud and <u>underline</u> the short vowel sounds.

1. The cat sat on the mat.
2. The pen is on the desk.
3. It is a sunny day.
4. The top is on the shelf.
5. The cup is full of water.

A Day at the Farm

The sun was hot at the farm. Ann got a cup of water. Ben fed the hens in the pen. The cat sat on a mat by the barn. The pup ran and had fun. Pat had a hat on his head. He threw a ball to Jim. Jim then hit it with a bat. A frog hopped away from the ball.

The pigs were in the mud. The dog dug a big pit. The cat and the dog were friends. The cat spotted a rat. It ran after the rat. The kids saw a lot of hens. A hen laid an egg in the pen. Ben put the egg in a box.

The farmer had a big red truck. The truck had a lot of hay. The kids liked to play on the hay. The dog sat on the truck and barked. The hens clucked in the pen. The sun went down and it got dark. The stars came out. The kids sat by the fire. It was a good day at the farm.

Comprehension Questions:

1. Where did Ben feed the hens?

____

2. What did Pat have on his head?

____

3. What did Ann get a cup of?

____

4. Where did the kids sit when it got dark?

____

5. What color was the farmer's truck?

____

A Trip to the Market

It was a sunny day. The sun was hot and bright. The market was busy. Pam had a list of items to buy. She got a pen to check off the list. The pup stayed at home.

At the market, Pam got a top for her son. She then bought a hat for her daughter. She also got some red pens for school. The kids had fun at the market. They saw a man with a big bag. Pam bought some eggs. The kids wanted some candy. Pam let them buy a small bag.

They put the items in the car. At home, the kids helped put the things away. Pam then made lunch for everyone. They sat and ate at the table. The dog sat by Pam's feet. The sun was still bright. The trip to the market was fun.

Comprehension Questions:

1. What did Pam buy for her son?

____

2. Where did the pup stay?

____

3. What did Pam buy for her daughter?

____

4. Where did the kids help put things away?

____

5. What did the kids want at the market?

____

At the Park

The park was full of kids. The sun was shining brightly. Sam had a bat and a ball. Tim had a big red kite. The kids ran and played. The cat sat on the mat. Sam's hat fell off the bench. The dog barked at the kite.

Jen had a cup of juice. She sat on the bench with her mom. She saw a pen on the ground. The dog ran after Sam's ball. Tim's kite flew high in the sky. The kids had fun in the sun. The park was a busy place. It was a good day for fun.

The kids played until it was dark. They sat on the mat and ate snacks. The dog was tired and slept. The pen was lost in the grass. The kite was put away. The hat was found under the bench. The cat was back at home. The day at the park was done.

Comprehension Questions:

1. What did Sam have at the park?

____

2. What did Jen have a cup of?

____

3. What did the dog run after?

____

4. Where was the pen lost?

____

5. Where was the hat found?

____

Exercise 6- Dictation

Your teacher will read some sentences from the texts above. Write them down.

____

____

____

____

Exercise 2

1. The c<u>a</u>t s<u>a</u>t <u>o</u>n the m<u>a</u>t.
2. The p<u>e</u>n <u>is</u> <u>o</u>n the d<u>e</u>sk.
3. <u>It</u> <u>is</u> <u>a</u> s<u>u</u>nny day.
4. The t<u>op</u> <u>is</u> <u>o</u>n the sh<u>e</u>lf.
5. The c<u>up</u> <u>is</u> f<u>u</u>ll <u>of</u> w<u>a</u>ter.

Exercise 3

1. Ben fed them in the pen.
2. Pat had a hat on his head.
3. Anna got a cup of water.
4. The kids sat by the fire.
5. The truck was red.

Exercise 4

1. She bought him a top.
2. The pup stayed at home.
3. She bought a hat for her daughter.
4. They helped put things away at home.
5. The kids wanted candy.

Exercise 5

1. Sam had a bat and a ball.
2. Jen had a cup of juice.
3. The dog ran after the ball.
4. The pen was lost in the grass.
5. The hat was found under the bench.

Let's reflect on your progress.

1.   What sounds did you review and practice?

2.   What reading skills did you practice?

3.   What strategies can you use to improve your reading comprehension skills?

4.   What do you want your instructor to know about your challenges?

LESSON 2

LONG VOWEL SOUNDS

Objectives:

1. Students will review and produce long vowel sounds.
2. Students will read short texts and answer comprehension questions correctly.

Exercise 1- Read and repeat the letters and sounds below.

Long Vowel	Examples
long a	make, take
long e	beet, feet
long i	tile, lime
long o	cope, tone
long u	music, cute
long oo	root, loop, droop

Exercise 2- Read the following sentences aloud and underline the long vowel sounds.

1. The brave snake was in the shade.
2. The beet is sweet and great to eat.
3. She can tie her shoes with ease.

4. The coat is blue and smooth.

5. He likes to play music on rainy days.

6. The goo is sticky and feels like glue.

Exercise 3- Read the text aloud before answering the questions.

A Day at the Lake

Jake and Kate went to the lake. The sun was bright, and the weather was great. They saw a boat with a white sail on the lake. They wanted to make a big sandcastle. Kate brought a rake to smooth the sand. Jake found a beetle in the sand. They took a break to eat some cake.

Later, they played with a kite. The kite flew high in the sky. They could see the kite's tail dance in the wind. They ran along the shore and found a long piece of rope. The boat came back to the dock. The sun began to set, making the sky orange and pink. They knew it was time to go home.

On their way home, they talked about the fun they had. Kate said she loved the lake. Jake agreed and said they should go back soon. They reached home and were very tired. They took off their shoes and sat down to rest. The memory of the lake made them smile. It was a perfect day. They hoped to have many more days like this.

Comprehension Questions:

1. What did Jake and Kate want to make at the lake?

____

2. What did Kate bring to smooth the sand?

____

3. What flew high in the sky?

____

4. What did they find along the shore?

____

5. What colors did the sky turn when the sun set?

____

A Visit to the Zoo

The zoo was a place full of excitement. Sue and Lee went to see the animals. The first animal they saw was a huge elephant. It had a long trunk and big ears. They took pictures of the elephant. Next, they saw a lion lying in the sun. The lion looked very calm and relaxed. They moved on to see more animals.

Sue wanted to see the monkeys. They found the monkeys swinging on ropes. The monkeys made funny faces at Sue and Lee. They laughed and took more pictures. Lee liked the zebras with their black and white stripes. The zoo had many different kinds of animals. They walked through the zoo, enjoying every moment.

Before leaving, they visited the gift shop. Sue bought a toy lion, and Lee chose a zebra shirt. They talked about their favorite animals on the way home. Sue loved the monkeys, while Lee's favorite was the lion. The trip to the zoo was exciting and fun. They promised to visit the zoo again soon.

Comprehension Questions:

1. What was the first animal Sue and Lee saw at the zoo?

____

2. What did the monkeys do that made Sue and Lee laugh?

____

3. What did Lee like about the zebras?

____

4. What did Sue buy at the gift shop?

____

5. What was Lee's favorite animal at the zoo?

____

Music Class

Music class was always exciting. Ms. June was the music teacher. She taught the students to sing and play instruments. They learned to play the flute and the piano. Last Saturday, they learned a new song. The song had a lot of high notes. It was a bit challenging, but they enjoyed it. The class sang together and sounded great.

Ms. June also showed them how to read music notes. She explained what each note meant. The students practiced reading the notes. They played a simple tune on their flutes. Ms. June encouraged them to practice every day. She said practice makes perfect. The students were eager to improve their skills.

At the end of the class, they had a small performance. Each student played a short piece on their instrument. The parents were invited to watch. Everyone clapped and cheered. Ms. June was very proud of her students. The music class was a big success. The students looked forward to the next class.

Comprehension Questions:

1. Who was the music teacher?

____

2. What instruments did the students learn to play?

____

3. What did the students learn about music notes?

____

4. What did the students do at the end of the class?

____

5. How did the teacher feel about her students?

____

Exercise 6- Dictation

Your teacher will read some sentences from the texts above. Write them down.

____

____

____

____

____

Exercise 2

1. The br**a**ve sn**a**ke was in the sh**a**de.
2. The b**ee**t is sw**ee**t and gr**ea**t to **ea**t.
3. Sh**e** can t**ie** her sh**oe**s with **ea**se.
4. The c**oa**t is bl**ue** and sm**oo**th.
5. He l**i**kes to pl**ay** m**u**sic on r**ai**ny d**ay**s.
6. The g**oo** is sticky and f**ee**ls l**i**ke gl**ue**.

Exercise 3

1. They wanted to make a big sandcastle.
2. She brought a rake.
3. A kite flew high.
4. They found a long piece of rope.
5. The sky turned orange and pink.

Exercise 4

1. They saw a huge elephant first.
2. The monkeys made funny faces.
3. He liked their black and white stripes.
4. Sue bought a toy lion.
5. Lee's favorite animal was the lion.

Exercise 5

1. Ms. June was the music teacher.
2. The students learned to play the flute and the piano.
3. The students learned what each note meant and how to read them.
4. They had a small performance where each student played a short piece on their instrument.
5. Ms. June felt very proud.

Let's reflect on your progress.

1. What sounds did you review and practice?

2. What reading skills did you practice?

3. What strategies can you use to improve your reading comprehension skills?

4. What do you want your instructor to know about your challenges?

LESSON 3

SPECIAL VOWEL SOUNDS

Objectives:

1. Students will review and produce special vowel sounds.
2. Students will read short texts with special vowel sounds and answer comprehension questions correctly.

Exercise 1- Read and repeat the letters and sounds below.

Special Vowel Sounds	Examples
aw	law, claw
oi	oil, toy
ow	owl, ouch
ow	flow, yellow
ey	they, grey
ew	new, few
oo (short)	book, cook

ai	rain, train
oa	boat, coat
ei	vein, reign
ea	sea, leaf
ea	spread, wealth
ie	pie, tie
ie	brief, chief
oe	toe, foe
ou	out, house

Exercise 2- Read the following sentences aloud and <u>underline</u> the special vowel sounds.

1. She heard a noise outside the house.
2. Kyle hit his elbow when he fell down.
3. The boys found a coin at the park.
4. The new book is on the table by the coat.
5. The cook prepared a delicious meal.
6. The rain fell on the train as it passed the station.
7. The boat peacefully glides over the waves.
8. The veil covered her face and smile.
9. The pie is on the plate and ready to be served.
10. The toe is part of the foot and helps with balance.

A Rainy-Day Adventure

It was a rainy day, and the kids were stuck inside. They decided to play with their toys. Jenny found an old toy boat. She filled the sink with water and sailed the boat. Tom had a book about owls. He read it to his sister. They heard a loud sound and looked outside. A real owl was sitting on a branch. It was wet from the rain.

The rain continued to pour. Jenny and Tom put on their raincoats. They went outside to jump in puddles. The water splashed everywhere. They saw a train pass by in the distance. The train looked shiny in the rain. They played until they were soaked. They laughed and had a lot of fun.

After playing, they went back inside. Their mom had made some hot cocoa. They sat by the window and watched the rain. The toy boat was still floating in the sink. The owl had flown away. Jenny and Tom talked about their adventure. It was a great rainy day.

Comprehension Questions:

1. What did Jenny and Tom do when they were stuck inside?

____

2. Where did Jenny sail the toy boat?

____

3. What animal did Tom read about?

____

4. What did they do outside in the rain?

____

5. What did their mom make for them after playing outside?

____

A Trip to the Farm

Sam and his family went to visit a farm. They saw many animals. There were cows, goats, and sheep. Sam's favorite animal was the cow. He liked the sound it made. They then walked to the barn. It smelled like fresh hay. They saw hay bales. Sam climbed on the hay and pretended to be a farmer.

They walked to the pond and saw ducks swimming. The water was calm, and the ducks looked happy. Sam threw some bread into the pond. The ducks quacked and swam to eat the bread. They saw a goat playing with a toy. The goat was funny and made everyone laugh. They took pictures with the animals.

Before leaving, they visited the farm shop. They bought fresh eggs and milk. Sam also got a new book about farms. The family thanked the farmer and went home. Sam talked about the animals all the way home. It was a fun trip to the farm. He wanted to visit again soon.

Comprehension Questions:

1. What was Sam's favorite animal at the farm?

____

2. What did Sam climb on in the barn?

____

3. What did Sam throw into the pond?

____

4. What did the goat play with?

____

5. What did they buy at the farm shop?

____

The New School

Lily was nervous about her first day at the new school. She wore her favorite coat and new shoes. She walked to the bus stop with her mom. The bus arrived, and she got on. She sat by the window and looked outside. The bus passed by a house with a big oak tree. She saw a crow sitting on a branch. The ride was long, but she enjoyed the view.

When she arrived at school, she saw many kids. They all looked friendly. Her teacher, Mrs. Green, welcomed her. She showed Lily her seat. The classroom had wide windows and colorful posters. Lily liked the classroom. She sat down and took out her books. The teacher started the lesson.

During recess, Lily made new friends. They played on the swings and slides. She shared her lunch with a girl named Zoe. They talked about their favorite books. Zoe liked the same books as Lily. They promised to sit together at lunch the next day. Lily felt happy and excited about her new school.

Comprehension Questions:

1. How did Lily feel about her first day at the new school?

   ____

2. What did Lily see on her way to school?

   ____

3. Who welcomed Lily to her new classroom?

   ____

4. What did Lily do during recess?

   ____

5. Who did Lily make friends with during recess?

   ____

Exercise 6- Dictation

Your teacher will read some sentences from the texts above. Write them down.

   ____

   ____

Exercise 2

1. She heard a n**oi**se **ou**ts**i**de the h**ou**se.
2. Kyle hit his elb**ow** when he fell d**ow**n.
3. The b**oy**s f**ou**nd a c**oi**n at the park.
4. The n**ew** b**oo**k is on the table by the c**oa**t.
5. The c**oo**k prepared a delicious m**ea**l.
6. The r**ai**n fell on the tr**ai**n as it passed the st**a**tion.
7. The b**oa**t p**ea**cefully gl**i**des over the w**a**ves.
8. The v**ei**l covered her f**a**ce and sm**i**le.
9. The p**ie** is on the pl**a**te and r**ea**dy to be served.
10. The t**oe** is part of the f**oo**t and helps with balance.

Exercise 3

1. They played with their toys.
2. She sailed it in the sink with water.
3. Tom read about owls.
4. They jumped in puddles.
5. She made hot cocoa.

Exercise 4

1. Sam's favorite animal was the cow.
2. Sam climbed on the hay bales.
3. He threw bread into the pond.
4. The goat played with a toy.
5. They bought fresh eggs and milk.

Exercise 5

1. Lily felt nervous.
2. She saw a crow on a branch.
3. Mrs. Green welcomed Lily.
4. She played on the swings and slides.
5. She made friends with a girl named Zoe.

Let's reflect on your progress.

1. What sounds did you review and practice?

2. What reading skills did you practice?

3. What strategies can you use to improve your reading comprehension skills?

4. What do you want your instructor to know about your challenges?

LESSON 4

VOWEL SOUNDS WITH R

Objectives:

1. Students will review and produce vowel sounds with R.
2. Students will read short texts that include vowel sounds with R and answer comprehension questions accurately.

Exercise 1- Read and repeat the letters and sounds below.

Sound with R	Examples
ar	bark, dark
er	her, bird, fur
or	fork, pork, stork
ur	turn, burn, nurse
ire	fire, tire, hire
are	care, share, rare

Exercise 2- Read the following sentences aloud and <u>underline</u> the sounds with R.

1. The dog will bark at night under the stars.
2. Her colorful bird sings every morning.

3. Use a fork to eat the pork with some corn.
4. The nurse will turn on the light after dark.
5. The tire on the car became flat at the fire station.
6. We care for our pets and their welfare.

Exercise 3- Read the text aloud before answering the questions.

A Day in the Park

The park was full of fun activities. Children played on the swings and slides. A dog barked happily as it chased a ball. Birds sang in the trees, creating a peaceful atmosphere. Parents sat on benches, watching their kids play. Some families had picnics on the grass. The park was a great place to relax and enjoy nature. Everyone had a wonderful time.

In one corner of the park, a group of friends played a game of soccer. They ran back and forth, kicking the ball with excitement. The sun was shining, making the day warm and bright. Nearby, an artist painted a picture of the park. She captured the beauty of the trees and flowers. People stopped to admire her work.

As the day came to an end, the park slowly emptied. The dog stopped barking and lay down to rest. The birds flew back to their nests. Families packed up their picnic baskets and headed home. The artist finished her painting and smiled at her work. It had been a perfect day in the park.

Comprehension Questions:

1. What did the children do in the park?

____

2. How did the dog show it was happy?

____

3. What did the artist do in the park?

____

4. What did the birds do at the end of the day?

____

5. What did families do as they left the park?

____

The Farmer's Market

Every Saturday, the town hosted a farmer's market. The market was a favorite spot for the community. Farmers brought fresh produce to sell. People came to buy fruits and vegetables. These included apples, berries, and oranges. The market was a busy place with lots of activity. Children enjoyed the sweet taste of fresh fruit.

One vendor sold homemade jams and jellies. The jars were lined up in neat rows. Customers sampled the different flavors. Another stall had fresh bread and pastries. The smell of baked goods filled the air. The farmer's market was a treat for all the senses. Everyone left with bags full of goodies.

Near the end of the market, a musician played the guitar. People gathered to listen to the music. Children danced and clapped their hands. The musician's songs were cheerful and lively. It was the perfect way to end a trip to the farmer's market. The market brought joy to the whole town.

Comprehension Questions:

1. What did farmers bring to sell at the market?

____

2. What did children enjoy at the market?

____

3. What did the vendor sell in jars?

____

4. How did the market smell?

____

5. What happened near the end of the market?

____

The Campfire

Camping trips were always exciting. At night, everyone gathered around the campfire. The fire crackled and popped. It kept them warm in the cool night air. They roasted marshmallows and made s'mores. The taste was sweet and delicious. The campfire was the highlight of the trip.

Someone started to tell a ghost story. The children listened with wide eyes. The story was spooky and thrilling. The light from the fire flickered on their faces. They loved the excitement of the ghost story. After the story, they sang songs. The music echoed in the night.

As the fire burned low, it was time for bed. They put out the fire and crawled into their tents. The night was quiet and peaceful. The stars twinkled above them. The sound of the forest was calming. It was the perfect end to a fun day of camping. They all slept soundly, dreaming of more adventures.

Comprehension Questions:

1. What did they roast over the campfire?

____

2. What was the highlight of the trip?

____

3. What kind of story did someone tell?

____

4. What did they do after the story?

____

5. How did the night end for the campers?

____

Exercise 6- Dictation

Your teacher will read some sentences from the texts above. Write them down.

____

____

Exercise 2

1. The dog will b**ar**k at night under the st**ar**s.
2. H**er** col**or**ful b**ir**d sings every m**or**ning.
3. Use a f**or**k to eat the p**or**k with some c**or**n.
4. The nu**r**se will t**ur**n on the light aft**er** d**ar**k.
5. The t**ire** on the c**ar** became flat at the f**ire** station.
6. We c**are** f**or** our pets and their welf**are**.

Exercise 3

1. The children played on the swings and slides.
2. The dog barked happily while chasing a ball.
3. The artist painted a picture of the park.
4. The birds flew back to their nests.
5. Families packed up their picnic baskets and headed home.

Exercise 4

1. Farmers brought fresh produce.
2. Children enjoy the sweet taste of fresh fruit.
3. The vendor sold homemade jams and jellies.
4. The market smelled like baked goods.
5. A musician played the guitar.

Exercise 5

1. They roasted marshmallows over the fire.
2. The campfire was the highlight of the trip.
3. Someone told a ghost story.
4. They sang songs after the story.
5. They put out the fire, crawled into their tents and slept.

Let's reflect on your progress.

1.   What sounds did you review and practice?

2.   What reading skills did you practice?

3.   What strategies can you use to improve your reading comprehension skills?

4.   What do you want your instructor to know about your challenges?

LESSON 5

THE CONSONANT SOUNDS

Objectives:

1. Students will review and produce the consonant sounds in words and sentences.
2. Students will read short texts that include the consonant sounds and accurately answer questions based on the texts.

Exercise 1- Read aloud and repeat the letters and sounds below.

Letters	Examples
b	**b**ed, **b**ad
k	**c**at, **k**ick
d	**d**og, **d**ip
f	**f**an, **f**ig
g	**g**ot, **g**irl
h	**h**as, **h**im
j	**j**ob, **j**oke
l	**l**id, **l**ove
m	**m**op, **m**ath

n	not, nice
p	pan, play
r	ran, rake
s	sit, smile
t	to, take
v	van, vine
w	water, winter
x	relax, next
y	yellow, yawn
z	zipper, zap

1. The bed is big with blue blankets.

2. The cat can kick the cushion.

3. The dog dips his paw into the dish.

4. The fig is fresh from the tree.

5. The girl got a gift for her birthday.

6. He has a heavy hat on his head.

7. The joke was about a job in the jungle.

8. The lid covers the large pot.

9. The mop is used to clean the messy room.

10. It is not nice to be noisy at night.

11. The pan is used to make fluffy pancakes.

12. He ran for the red garden rake.

13. She sits and smiles sweetly in the van.

14. They went to take a nap in the cozy nook.

15. The vine grew along the van's side.

16. The water in the pool is cool.

17. The yellow bird loves the warm sun.

18. The visitors looked at the zebra in the zoo.

19. She found a new job in a quiet town.

20. They traveled to the countryside in a van.

Exercise 3- Read the text aloud before answering the questions.

A Visit to the Zoo

The sun was shining brightly. The zoo was full of animals. The big bear was sleeping in its den. The monkeys were swinging on branches. The giraffe was eating leaves from a tall tree. The elephant was spraying water from its trunk.

The kids were excited to see the different animals. A zookeeper was feeding the lions. The lions were roaring loudly. The job of a zookeeper is not easy. The zookeeper feeds the animals and cleans the enclosures. One was also feeding the birds. The door of a birdcage was open and a bird flew out quickly.

Visitors took pictures of the different animals. The water in the pond was clear and ducks were swimming in it. Nearby, a flamingo stood on one leg. The bear woke up and yawned. The monkeys made the children laugh with their antics. The zoo was a fun place to learn about animals. The kids had a great time. They hoped to come back soon.

Comprehension Questions:

1. What was the big bear doing?

____

2. Who was feeding the lions?

____

3. What happened when the lid of the cage was open?

____

4. What tasks do zookeepers do?

____

5. What animal was in the pond?

____

A Day at the Beach

The sun was shining brightly over the beach. The cat was playing with the sand. The dog was joyfully running along the shore. The girl was building a sandcastle when she found a seashell. The boy was flying a colorful kite that danced in the breeze. The van was parked near the water. The big waves were crashing against the shore.

Families were having picnics under the clear blue sky. Everyone shared a bowl full of food. A fat seagull was flying above and searching for its own food. The lid of the cooler was open. The ice was melting quickly. The kids went into the water to play. The water was cool and refreshing.

Everyone was enjoying the beach. Then, the sun began setting. The cat curled up on the beach towel. It began napping under the umbrella. The dog was busy digging a hole. The kids were tired but happy from the day's activities. The van was packed up and ready to go home. It had been a fun and memorable day at the beach.

Comprehension Questions:

1. What was the girl doing at the beach?

____

2. What was the boy flying?

____

3. Where was the van parked?

____

4. What was the fat seagull looking for?

____

5. What was everyone sharing?

____

A Trip to the Farm

The farm was a busy place. The cat was chasing a rat. The dog was guarding the sheep. Nearby, a hen was pecking at the ground and looking for grains. The pigs were rolling in the muddy pen. The girl was milking the cow while the boy was riding a horse. The farmer was feeding the animals.

Overhead, white clouds hid the sun. The boy began helping with the chores. He used the mop in the barn. The girl found a nest of eggs in the hay. The farmer put a pan of water on the stove. He also put water in the trough for the animals. He forgot to cover the feed bin. The dog was watching everyone closely.

Soon, the sun began setting. The farm was peaceful and quiet. The cat was napping on the hay. The dog was resting by the barn. The hen was roosting in the coop. The pig was sleeping soundly. The girl and boy were playing in the yard. The farmer was putting away his tools. The farm day was ending.

Comprehension Questions:

1. What was the cat chasing?

____

2. Who was guarding the sheep?

____

3. What did the girl find in the hay?

____

4. What did the farmer put in the trough?

____

5. What were the girl and boy doing at the end of the day?

____

Exercise 6- Dictation

Your teacher will read some sentences from the texts above. Write them down.

____

____

Exercise 2

1. The **bed** is **big** **w**ith **b**lue **blank**ets.
2. The **cat can kick** the **c**ushio**n**.
3. The **dog dips his paw** in**to** the **d**ish.
4. The **fig is f**resh **from** the **tr**ee.
5. The **girl g**o**t** a **gift fo**r **h**er **b**irth**day**.
6. **H**e **has** a **heavy hat** o**n his head**.
7. The **jo**ke **was** a**bout** a **job in** the **jung**le.
8. The **l**id **c**ove**rs** the **l**arge **pot**.
9. The **mop is** us**ed to cl**ea**n** the **messy** **r**oo**m**.
10. **It is not n**ice **to be n**oisy **at night**.
11. The **pan is** us**ed to m**ake **fl**uffy **p**an**c**ak**es**.
12. **H**e **ran f**or the **red g**ar**den r**ake.
13. She **sits a**n**d smiles sweet**ly **in** the **van**.
14. The**y went to t**ake a **nap in** the **c**oz**y noo**k.
15. The **vine grew** a**l**ong the **van's side**.
16. The **w**ater **in** the **pool is c**oo**l**.
17. The **yellow bird l**ov**es** the **w**arm **sun**.
18. The **visitors l**ook**ed at** the **zebra in** the **z**oo.
19. She **f**ou**nd** a **n**ew **job in** a quiet **town**.
20. They **trav**el**ed** to the **c**ou**ntryside in** a **van**.

Exercise 3

1. The big bear is sleeping.
2. The zookeeper was feeding the lions.
3. A bird flew out quickly.
4. Zookeepers feed the animals and clean the enclosures.
5. Ducks were in the pond.

Exercise 4

1. The girl was building a sandcastle.
2. The boy was flying a colorful kite.
3. The van was parked near the water.
4. The seagull was looking for food.
5. Everyone was sharing a bowl of food.

Exercise 5

1. The cat was chasing a rat.
2. The dog was guarding the sheep.
3. The girl found a nest of eggs in the hay.
4. The farmer put water in the trough.
5. The boy and girl were playing in the yard.

Let's reflect on your progress.

1. What sounds did you review and practice?

2. What reading skills did you practice?

3. What strategies can you use to improve your reading comprehension skills?

4. What do you want your instructor to know about your challenges?

SPECIAL CONSONANT SOUNDS (GROUP 1)

Objectives:

1. Students will review and produce special consonant sounds (two or three consonants combine their sounds) in words and sentences.
2. Students will read short texts that include these consonant sounds and answer questions based on the texts.

Exercise 1- Read aloud and repeat the letters and sounds below.

Letter	Examples
bl	**bl**ue, **bl**ow
br	**br**own, **br**eak
cl	**cl**ap, **cl**ose
cr	**cr**y, **cr**ust
dr	**dr**y, **dr**ag
fl	**fl**y, **fl**ip
fr	**fr**y, **fr**eeze
gl	**gl**ue, **gl**ove
gr	**gr**een, **gr**ound

pl	play, please
pr	prize, prank
sc	score, scarf
scr	scrub, scream
sk	skate, sky
sl	slip, slap
sm	smell, smile
sp	spot, speed
spl	splendid, splash
spr	spray, spring
squ	square, squeak
st	star, stop
str	stripe, strap
sw	sweet, sweater
tr	tree, try
tw	twist, twelve

Exercise 2- Read the following sentences aloud and <u>underline</u> the special consonant sounds.

1. The blue sky is clear and the birds are flying.
2. She will clap her hands on stage.
3. The fly landed on the flip-flop.
4. Use strong glue to fix the broken frame.
5. The friends like to play games.
6. The fluffy brown dog is cute and greets everyone.
11. She won a prize for her creative project.
12. Try to climb the branches of that tall tree.
13. They went to skate in their sweaters.
14. Be careful not to break the fragile vase.
15. The spot on the shirt is bright red.
16. Stop at the street corner before crossing.
17. The sweet candy is yummy and sticky.

7.   Do not cry over the crusty old bread.
8.   The towel dried quickly in the breezy weather.
9.   He likes to fry fish until it is crispy and golden.
10. The ground is wet and slippery.

18. Spray the plants with water to keep them green.
19. The stripe on the smelly shirt is blue.
20. The glue bottle has a small crack on it.

Exercise 3- Read the text aloud before answering the questions.

A Day at the Park

A group of friends went to the park. The sky was blue, and the sun was shining brightly. They set up their picnic area under a large tree. One girl found a quiet spot to sit and read her book. The others played a game of frisbee. The frisbee glided smoothly through the air.

After playing, they sat down for a snack. They had sandwiches and sweet treats packed. One friend had a blue drink, and another had a green one. They talked and laughed about their week. A girl showed her friend how to do a handstand and everyone clapped. A boy tried to do it but slipped and fell softly onto the grass. Everyone laughed and helped him up. They enjoyed their snack time together.

As the day ended, they cleaned up their spot. They packed their belongings and folded the blanket. They also picked up their trash and put it in the bin. The sky started to get dark, and it was time to go home. They waved goodbye to each other. The park was empty and quiet. The friends were tired but happy. They all looked forward to coming back another day. They had a great time at the park.

Comprehension Questions:

1.   Where did the friends set up their picnic?

____

2.   What color was the sky?

____

3.   What game did the friends play?

____

4.   What did they have for a snack?

____

5. What did they do with their trash?

____

A Visit to the Farmer's Market

On Saturday, we went to the farmer's market. There were many things to see and buy. We saw fresh fruits and vegetables. My mom bought some brown eggs and green beans. We walked past a stall that sold sweet honey. My sister loved the blue flowers she saw on sale at another stall. We also bought some fresh bread and cheese. The farmer's market was full of a variety of colors and smells.

At the market, we also saw a man playing a guitar. People stopped to listen to his music. Children clapped their hands and danced. My dad gave some money to the man. There was also a lady selling handmade gloves. My brother tried on a pair and liked them. My mom bought the gloves for him.

We stayed at the market until noon. After looking at the stalls, we ate lunch at a small café nearby. I had a sandwich and a drink. My sister had a slice of apple pie. After lunch, we strolled around some more. My dad bought a jar of strawberry jam before stalls began closing. The farmer's market was a fun place to be. We had a great time. It was a lovely way to spend the day.

Comprehension Questions:

1. What did the mom buy at the market?

____

2. Who was playing music at the market?

____

3. What did children do when they heard the music?

____

4. What did my brother try on?

____

5. Where did we eat lunch?

____

A Day at the Wildlife Reserve

A group of friends spent an afternoon at a wildlife reserve. They were excited to see the native animals. The weather was perfect as the sky was clear. They set off on a trail. On the way, they spotted deer grazing. Later, they saw a herd of bison in a field. Noah also saw a bald eagle perched on a tree. He showed the others.

While walking, the friends came across a river. The water was clear, and there were many kinds of fish swimming in it. The group also observed animals like squirrels and otters nearby. Sophia spotted a raccoon washing its paws in the water.

Afterward, the group enjoyed a picnic at the reserve. They had packed sandwiches, fruits, and snacks. They talked about what they saw and enjoyed the sounds of nature. The friends agreed they would return. The day was memorable and educational.

Comprehension Questions:

1. What animal did the group see grazing?

____

2. Where was the bald eagle?

____

3. What was swimming in the river?

____

4. What was the raccoon doing?

____

5. What did the group pack for their picnic?

____

Exercise 6- Dictation

Your teacher will read some sentences from the texts above. Write them down.

____

____

____

Exercise 2

1. The **bl**ue **sk**y is **cl**ear and the birds are **fl**ying.
2. She will **cl**ap her hands on **st**age.
3. The **fl**y landed on the **fl**ip-**fl**op.
4. Use **str**ong **gl**ue to fix the **br**oken **fr**ame.
5. The **fr**iends like to **pl**ay games.
6. The **fl**uffy **br**own dog is cute and **gr**eets everyone.
7. Do not **cr**y over the **cr**usty old **br**ead.
8. The towel **dr**ied quickly in the **br**eezy weather.
9. He likes to **fr**y fish until it is **cr**ispy and golden.
10. The **gr**ound is wet and **sl**ippery.
11. She won a **pr**ize for her **cr**eative **pr**oject.
12. **Tr**y to **cl**imb the **br**anches of that tall **tr**ee.
13. They went to **sk**ate in their **sw**eaters.
14. Be careful not to **br**eak the **fr**agile vase.
15. The **sp**ot on the shirt is **br**ight red.
16. **St**op at the **str**eet corner before **cr**ossing.
17. The **sw**eet candy is yummy and **st**icky.
18. **Spr**ay the **pl**ants with water to keep them **gr**een.
19. The **str**ipe on the **sm**elly shirt is **bl**ue.
20. The **gl**ue bottle has a **sm**all **cr**ack on it.

Exercise 3

1. They set up under a large tree.
2. The sky was blue.
3. They played a game of frisbee.
4. They had sandwiches and sweet treats.
5. They put the trash in the bin.

Exercise 4

1. Mom bought brown eggs and green beans.
2. A man was playing a guitar.
3. The children clapped their hands and danced.
4. He tried on handmade gloves.
5. We ate lunch at a small café nearby.

Exercise 5

1. They saw deer grazing.
2. The bald eagle was perched on a tree.
3. Many kinds of fish were swimming in the river.
4. The raccoon was washing its paws in the water.
5. They packed sandwiches, fruits, and snacks.

Let's reflect on your progress.

1. What sounds did you review and practice?

2. What reading skills did you practice?

3. What strategies can you use to improve your reading comprehension skills?

4. What do you want your instructor to know about your challenges?

LESSON 7

SPECIAL CONSONANT SOUNDS (GROUP 2)

Objectives:

1. Students will review and produce special consonant sounds (two consonants make a new sound) in words and sentences.
2. Students will read short texts that include these consonant sounds and answer questions based on the texts.

Exercise 1- Read aloud and repeat the letters and sounds below.

Sounds	Examples
ch	chin, ouch
sh	ship, push
th	thing, this
th	other, them
wh	when, where
gn	gnome, sign
kn	knee, know
gh	ghost, laugh
ph	phone, graph

45

Exercise 2- Read the following sentences aloud and <u>underline</u> the special consonant sounds listed in Exercise 1.

1. The ship will push through the water in the storm.
2. This thing is very important for the team.
3. Do you know when you will come home?
4. The artist designed the sign hanging outside.
5. He felt a sharp pain and knew he hurt his knee.
6. The ghost at the party made everyone laugh.
7. I will call you on the phone to discuss the graph.
8. The chef cut the chicken with a sharp knife.
9. When are you visiting the new park?
10. I pushed the shopping cart through the store.

Exercise 3- Read the text aloud before answering the questions.

The Mysterious Forest

The forest was dark and quiet. Oliver and Lucas heard a creepy laugh from the trees. A gnome stood near a sign that read, "Beware." They walked past the gnome with caution. They saw a ship on a lake in the distance. The moonlight made the lake shine. Suddenly, they heard a noise and Oliver said, "Ouch!" A branch had fallen from a tree and hit him.

They continued following the path. Their knees were shaking with fear. A shadow moved, and they saw a ghost. The ghost floated near the trees. The boys became scared. They knew they had to leave quickly. They ran back to the entrance of the forest.

When they reached the entrance, they spotted a phone booth. They called their friends to tell them about the ghost. Their friends laughed and explained that it was just a trick. Oliver and Lucas decided to come back during the day. The mysterious forest was not as scary in the sunlight.

Comprehension Questions:

1. Why did Oliver say, "Ouch!"?

____

2. What did the sign read near the gnome?

____

3. How did the boys feel in the forest?

____

4.   What did they see near the trees?

____

5.   Why did they call their friends?

____

The Science Fair

The science fair was full of exciting projects. One student built a phone from scratch. Another displayed a graph showing the growth of plants. The ship model in the corner caught everyone's attention. The student explained how ships float. The judges were impressed with the projects. They took notes on their clipboards.

A girl showed her project about ghosts. She explained how people see ghosts in old houses. The judges asked questions about her research. A boy demonstrated how to use a phone app he created. The app could solve difficult math problems. The judges were amazed at his skill. They wrote down their comments.

At the end of the fair, the judges announced the winners. The phone project won first place. The ship model won second place. The ghost project won third place. Everyone cheered for the winners. They proudly took pictures with their projects. The science fair was a huge success. They all looked forward to next year's fair.

Comprehension Questions:

1.   What did one student build from scratch?

____

2.   What did the graph show?

____

3.   What did the girl's project explain?

____

4.   What could the boy's phone app do?

____

5.   Who won first place at the science fair?

____

The Camping Trip

Mark and David went on a camping trip in the mountains. They packed a phone in case of emergencies. The tent was set up near a stream. They saw a sign that read, "Beware of bears." The night was chilly, and they made a fire. They cooked food and shared stories. They heard an owl hoot in the distance.

In the morning, they went for a hike. They saw a gnome statue hidden among the trees. They laughed at its funny face. The trail was steep, and their knees hurt from climbing. They reached the top and saw a beautiful view. They took pictures and rested for a while. They decided to head back to the camp.

When they returned, they found a storybook about ghosts. They read it by the fire. The story was about a haunted ship. They heard a noise and saw a shadow. They were scared, but then they realized it was the wind. They laughed and continued reading. The camping trip was full of adventures.

Comprehension Questions:

1. Where did they set up their tent?

____

2. What did the sign read near the camp?

____

3. What did they see hidden among the trees?

____

4. What hurt from climbing the steep trail?

____

5. What was the storybook about?

____

Exercise 6- Dictation

Your teacher will read some sentences from the texts above. Write them down.

____

____

Exercise 2

1. **The** **sh**ip will pu**sh** **th**rough **the** water in **the** storm.
2. **Th**is **th**ing is very important for **the** team.
3. Do you **kn**ow **wh**en you will come home?
4. **The** artist desi**gn**ed the si**gn** hanging outside.
5. He felt a **sh**arp pain and **kn**ew he hurt his **kn**ee.
6. **The** **gh**ost at **the** party made everyone lau**gh**.
7. I will call you on **the** **ph**one to discuss **the** gra**ph**.
8. **The** **ch**ef cut **the** **ch**icken with a **sh**arp **kn**ife.
9. **Wh**en are you visiting **the** new park?
10. I pu**sh**ed **the** **sh**opping cart **th**rough **the** store.

Exercise 3

1. A branch fell and hit Oliver.
2. The sign read, "Beware."
3. The boys felt scared.
4. They saw a ghost.
5. They called their friends to tell them about the ghost.

Exercise 4

1. They built a phone.
2. The graph showed the growth of plants.
3. Her project explained how people see ghosts in old houses.
4. His app could solve difficult math problems.
5. The student who built the phone project won first place.

Exercise 5

1. They set up their tent near a stream.
2. The sign read, "Beware of bears."
3. They saw a gnome statue.
4. Their knees hurt.
5. The book was about a haunted ship.

Let's reflect on your progress.

1. What sounds did you review and practice?

2. What reading skills did you practice?

3. What strategies can you use to improve your reading comprehension skills?

4. What do you want your instructor to know about your challenges?

LESSON 8

VOCABULARY AND SOUNDS

Objectives:

1. Students will choose appropriate words to complete the sentences given.
2. Students will practice reading sentences aloud to improve their pronunciation and increase their awareness of sounds in English.

Exercise 1- Workplace and Community Resources: Fill in the blanks with the correct words (*center, take, make, name, start*). Then, read each sentence aloud.

1. The community _____________________ offers many resources for job seekers.
2. Please sign your _____________________ at the end of the document.
3. The manager will _____________________ a break after the meeting.
4. The employee will _____________________ the project next week.
5. The nurse will _____________________ sure you are comfortable.

Exercise 2- Job Search: Fill in the blanks with the correct words (*review, resume, apply, eight, communication*). Then, read each sentence aloud.

1. She will _____________________ for the job online.
2. The interview is scheduled for _____________________ o'clock.
3. He needs to update his _____________________ before applying.
4. The employer will _____________________ all the applications.
5. It is important to have good _____________________ skills during an interview.

Exercise 3- Effective Communication: Fill in the blanks with the correct words (*check, phone, when, speak, speaking*). Then, read each sentence aloud.

1. It is important to _______________________ clearly during a job interview.
2. Please _______________________ your email for updates.
3. Effective communication involves both _______________________ and listening.
4. _______________________ will the meeting start?
5. The _______________________ rang loudly in the office.

Exercise 4- Financial Literacy: Fill in the blanks with the correct words (*save, purchase, invest, offer, price*). Then, read each sentence aloud.

1. She needs to _______________________ money for her future.
2. The _______________________ was too good to pass up.
3. The _______________________ of the item is within our budget.
4. He will _______________________ in the stock market.
5. The _______________________ will be delivered next week.

Exercise 5- Health Care Services: Fill in the blanks with the correct words (*patient, congenital, diet, diagnosis, appointment*). Then, read each sentence aloud.

1. The _______________________ is scheduled for tomorrow morning.
2. The _______________________ was given by the eye specialist.
3. The _______________________ needs to stay hydrated and rest.
4. The _______________________ heart condition requires regular check-ups.
5. The doctor recommended a balanced _______________________ for better health.

Exercise 6- Dictation

Your teacher will read some sentences. Write down what you hear.

____

____

____

____

____

Exercise 7- Complete the following sentences.

1. The bank that I like is____
2. Health insurance is essential because _________________________________
3. Having a good job is important because _______________________________
4. Managing money well means ____
5. To stay healthy, I ____
6. To save money, I ____

Answer Keys

Exercise 1- Answer Key:

1. center
2. name
3. take
4. start
5. make

Exercise 2- Answer Key:

1. apply
2. eight
3. resume
4. review
5. communication

Exercise 3- Answer Key:

1. speak
2. check
3. speaking
4. when
5. phone

Exercise 4- Answer Key:

1. save
2. offer
3. price
4. invest
5. purchase

Exercise 5- Answer Key:

1. appointment
2. diagnosis
3. patient
4. congenital
5. diet

Let's reflect on your progress.

1. What sounds did you review and practice?

2. What reading skills did you practice?

3. What strategies can you use to improve your reading comprehension skills?

4. What do you want your instructor to know about your challenges?

READING ALOUD AND COMPREHENSION QUESTIONS

Objectives:

1. Students will read aloud various texts on practical life skills.
2. Students will answer comprehension questions based on these texts.

Exercise 1- Read the text aloud before answering the questions.

Ensuring Safety in the Workplace

Workplace safety is essential for protecting employees. Every worker must be aware of safety procedures. Wearing protective gear is crucial in hazardous environments. This gear includes helmets, gloves, and safety glasses. Employers must provide the necessary safety tools. Workers should use these tools correctly and consistently. Regular maintenance of equipment prevents accidents.

Implementing safety measures is a shared responsibility. Supervisors should conduct regular safety inspections. This helps identify potential hazards early. It is also vital to keep walkways clear of obstructions. Slips and trips are common workplace accidents. Employees should be vigilant and cautious. Safety signs should be prominently displayed. These signs provide critical safety information. It is also important to report any unsafe conditions immediately. Regular feedback from employees can improve safety procedures. Everyone's participation is key to maintaining a safe workplace.

Emergency preparedness is another crucial aspect. Employees should know the location of emergency exits. They should also know how to respond to different emergencies. This includes fires, chemical spills, and medical emergencies. Employees should be able to use fire extinguishers and first aid kits. These kits should be easily accessible. Workers should also be trained in basic first aid. Communication during emergencies is vital. Having a clear evacuation plan can save lives. Regular emergency drills ensure everyone knows their role. Employers should review and update safety plans regularly. Keeping a record of safety incidents can help improve procedures. Continuous improvement is necessary for workplace safety. Training sessions should be conducted periodically. A safe workplace boosts employee morale and productivity.

Comprehension Questions:

1. Why is workplace safety important?

____

2. What protective gear should employees wear in hazardous environments?

____

3. How can regular maintenance of equipment help?

____

4. What is the role of supervisors in workplace safety?

____

5. Why is it important to keep walkways clear of obstructions?

____

6. What should employees be able to use in emergencies?

____

7. Summarize each paragraph in your own words.

____

The Importance of Effective Communication

Effective communication is crucial in any organization. It ensures that everyone understands their roles and responsibilities. Active listening is an essential part of communication. This means paying attention to the speaker and responding appropriately. Employees should use polite and professional language. Nonverbal communication, like body language, also plays a role. These include maintaining eye contact and nodding to show understanding. Written communication should be clear and concise. Emails and reports should be free of errors. Clear communication helps avoid misunderstandings.

Barriers to communication can hinder productivity. These barriers include language differences and noise. Technical jargon can also cause confusion. Simplifying the message can help. It is important to ensure that everyone understands the information. Visual aids like charts and diagrams can also be helpful. They make complex information easier to understand. Regular team meetings and training in communication skills can be beneficial. Feedback from team members is also valuable. This training should cover both verbal and nonverbal communication. Encouraging open communication creates a positive work environment. Employees should feel comfortable sharing their ideas and concerns.

Technology has changed the way we communicate. Emails, instant messaging, and video calls are common. It is important to use these tools effectively. Emails should be checked regularly. Instant messaging can be useful for quick communication. Video calls are great for remote meetings. However, face-to-face communication is still important. It builds stronger relationships. Balancing different communication methods is key. Understanding the preferences of team members can improve communication. Continuous improvement in communication practices ensures the organization runs smoothly.

Comprehension Questions:

1. Why is effective communication important in an organization?

____

2. What is active listening?

____

3. How can visual aids help in communication?

____

4. What are some barriers to communication mentioned in the text?

____

5. What can instant messaging be used for?

____

6. Why is face-to-face communication still important?

____

7. Summarize each paragraph in your own words.

____

Managing Your Household Budget

Managing a household budget is essential for financial stability. Start by listing all sources of income. These include salaries, bonuses, and any other earnings. Next, list all monthly expenses. These can include rent, utilities, groceries, and transportation. It's important to differentiate between needs and wants. Needs are essential, while wants are optional. Tracking your spending can help identify unnecessary expenses. Budgeting apps can be useful tools. They can help you stay organized. Setting financial goals is also important. These can include saving for a vacation or paying off debt.

Credit cards can be a useful financial tool. However, they should be used responsibly. Only charge what you can afford to pay off each month. This helps avoid interest charges and debt. Always pay your credit card bill on time. Late payments can harm your credit score. It's also important to check your credit card statements regularly. Look for any unauthorized charges. Report them to your credit card company immediately. Using rewards programs can be beneficial. They can offer cash back or travel points. However, don't overspend just to earn rewards.

Building an emergency fund is essential. This fund should cover at least three to six months of expenses. In this way, it can be used in case of unexpected events. Regularly saving a portion of your income can help build this fund. Cutting back on non-essential expenses can also help. Regularly reviewing and adjusting your budget is important. This ensures that it reflects your current financial situation. Seeking advice from a financial advisor can be beneficial. They can provide personalized recommendations. Managing your budget and credit cards wisely can lead to financial security.

Comprehension Questions:

1. Why is managing a household budget important?

____

2. What is the difference between needs and wants?

____

3. How can budgeting apps be useful?

____

4. What is a key strategy for using credit cards responsibly?

____

5. Why is it important to build an emergency fund?

____

6. How can a financial advisor help with managing finances?

____

7. Summarize each paragraph in your own words.

____

Understanding US Elections

Elections in the United States are a fundamental part of democracy. Citizens have the right to vote for their leaders. The election process includes several steps. It begins with the nomination of candidates. These candidates represent different political parties. Campaigning is an essential part of elections. Candidates present their policies and goals to the public. Debates are held to discuss important issues. Voters are encouraged to learn about the candidates. This helps them make informed decisions.

Voting can be done in various ways. Many people vote in person at polling stations. Others use mail-in ballots or early voting options. It's important to register to vote before the election. Registration ensures that you are eligible to vote. On election day, polling stations are open from morning to evening. Voters are required to show identification. This process helps prevent fraud. After voting, ballots are counted. The results are announced publicly.

The outcome of the election impacts the entire country. Elected leaders make important decisions. These decisions affect laws, policies, and public services. It's important for citizens to participate in elections. Voting is a way to express your opinions. It's also a civic duty. Staying informed about political issues is essential. This helps you understand the implications of your vote. Elections are held at local, state, and national levels. Each level has different responsibilities. Participating in all levels of elections is important.

Comprehension Questions:

1. What is the first step in the election process?

____

2. Why are debates held during elections?

____

3. What are some ways people can vote?

____

4. Why is voter registration important?

____

5. How does the outcome of an election impact the country?

____

6. Why is it important for citizens to participate in elections?

____

7. Summarize each paragraph in your own words.

____

Civic Responsibilities in the United States

Citizens and residents of the United States have various responsibilities. One of the most important ones is obeying the law. Laws are in place to ensure order and safety. For example, discrimination and harassment are against the law. Everyone has the right to freedom and equality. It's important to respect the rights of others.

Voting is a fundamental responsibility. It allows citizens to choose their leaders. Everyone should stay informed about political issues. This helps you make educated voting decisions. Paying taxes is another key responsibility. Taxes fund public services like schools and roads. Therefore, it's important to file your taxes accurately and on time. Serving on a jury is also a civic duty. Jury service helps ensure a fair legal system. Citizens may be called for jury duty at any time.

Respecting your environment and community is another responsibility. This includes recycling and conserving resources for future generations. Participating in community activities is another responsibility. This can include volunteering and attending local meetings. Community involvement helps improve your neighborhood. Supporting the community by shopping locally is also beneficial. It helps local businesses thrive. Being a responsible citizen also means helping others. This can include donating to charities or assisting neighbors. Civic responsibilities ensure a strong and healthy society. Everyone's participation is essential.

Comprehension Questions:

1. Why is obeying the law important?

____

2. What do taxes fund?

____

3. What is the purpose of serving on a jury?

____

4. Why is staying informed about political issues important?

____

5. What are two community activities people can participate in?

____

6. What are some ways to respect the environment?

____

7. Summarize each paragraph in your own words.

____

Exercise 6- Read the text aloud before answering the questions.

Job Search and Interview Preparation

Looking for a job can be a challenging process. The first step is to create a strong resume. Your resume should highlight your skills and experience. Tailoring your resume for each job application is important. This shows employers that you are a good fit. Networking can also help in your job search. Connecting with professionals in your field can lead to job opportunities. Online job boards and company websites are useful resources. They provide a list of available positions.

Preparing for an interview is crucial. Research the company and the job role. This shows the employer that you are interested. Practice common interview questions and answers. Dressing appropriately is important. It creates a positive first impression. Arriving on time for the interview is essential. It shows that you are punctual and reliable. During the interview, listen carefully to the questions. Answer clearly and confidently. It's also important to ask questions about the role and the company.

After the interview, follow up with a thank-you note. This shows appreciation for the opportunity. It also keeps you in the employer's mind. Reflect on your interview performance. Think about what went well and what can be improved. Continue applying for jobs and attending interviews. Persistence is key to finding the right job. Staying positive and motivated is important. Job searching can take time, but with preparation and effort, you can succeed.

Comprehension Questions:

1. What should your resume highlight?

____

2. How can networking help in your job search?

____

3. Why is researching the company important before an interview?

____

4. What should you do to create a positive first impression during an interview?

____

5. Why is it important to follow up after an interview?

____

6. What should you reflect on after an interview?

____

7. Summarize each paragraph in your own words.

____

Understanding Federal Income and Sales Taxes

Federal income taxes are a major source of revenue for the government. They are collected from individuals and businesses. The amount of tax you pay depends on your income. Higher-income earners pay a higher percentage. Filing your tax return is an annual responsibility. It's important to report all sources of income. Deductions and credits can reduce your taxable income. These can include education expenses and charitable donations. Filing taxes accurately is essential to avoid penalties.

Sales taxes are collected on the sale of goods and services. They are usually a percentage of the purchase price. Sales tax rates vary by state and locality. Retailers are responsible for collecting sales tax. The collected tax is then sent to the government. Sales taxes fund local services like schools and public safety. It's important to keep records of your purchases. This helps ensure that sales taxes are paid correctly. Some states have tax holidays for certain items. These are periods when sales tax is not charged.

Understanding taxes helps you manage your finances better. Budgeting for taxes is important. Setting aside money throughout the year can help. Seeking advice from a tax professional can be beneficial. They can help you understand tax laws and find deductions. Staying informed about tax changes is also important. Tax laws can change, impacting how much you owe. Keeping accurate records makes tax filing easier. Proper tax management is crucial for financial stability.

Comprehension Questions:

1. What are federal income taxes used for?

____

2. How is the amount of federal income tax determined?

____

3. What are some examples of deductions and credits?

____

4. Who is responsible for collecting sales tax?

5. What do sales taxes fund?

6. Why is it important to keep records of your purchases?

7. Summarize each paragraph in your own words.

Exercise 8- Read the text aloud before answering the questions.

Navigating Health Care Services and Insurance

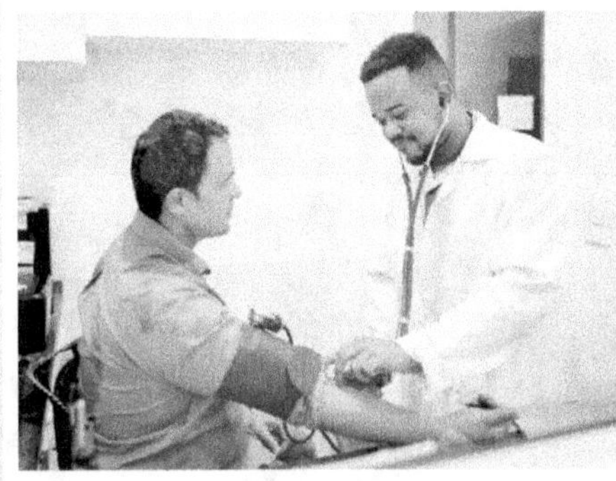

Healthcare services are essential for maintaining good health. They include visits to doctors, hospitals, and clinics. Preventive care is important for early detection of health issues. It includes check-ups, screenings and vaccinations. These can prevent serious illnesses.

Health insurance helps cover the cost of these services. There are different types of health insurance plans. They vary in coverage and cost. Choosing the right plan is important for your needs. Know what services are covered and what are not. This includes understanding co-pays and deductibles. A co-pay is a fixed amount you pay for a service. A deductible is the amount you pay before insurance covers the rest. Keeping track of your medical bills is important. It helps ensure that you are not overcharged. Contacting your insurance provider can clarify any doubts. They can explain your benefits and coverage.

Access to health care services can vary based on location. Some areas have more providers than others. It's important to know where to go in an emergency. Having a primary care doctor can help manage your health. They provide regular check-ups and referrals to specialists. Understanding the services available to you can improve your overall well-being. Staying informed about changes in health care laws is also important. This can affect your coverage and costs. Being proactive about your health ensures a better quality of life.

Comprehension Questions:

1. What are health care services?

2. Why is preventive care important?

____

3. What does health insurance help with?

____

4. What are co-pays and deductibles?

____

5. Why is it important to keep track of your medical bills?

____

6. How can having a primary care doctor help?

____

7. Summarize each paragraph in your own words.

____

Safely Using Medication

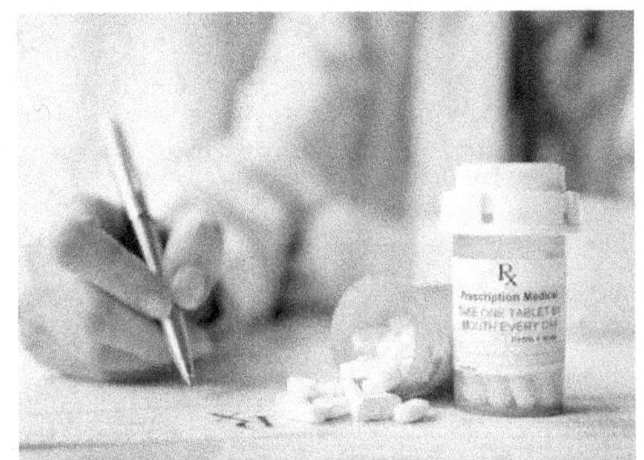

Taking medication as prescribed is crucial to treat health conditions effectively. Follow the doctor's instructions carefully. This includes the correct dosage and timing. Never take more or less than prescribed. Using a pill organizer can help you keep track. Always read the medication label for important instructions and information. For example, some medications should not be taken with certain foods or drinks. It is also important to know the side effects of your medication. Report any unusual symptoms to your doctor.

Storing medication properly is important. Keep it in a cool, dry place away from children. Some medications need to be refrigerated. Check the expiration date before use. Do not use expired medication. Disposing of medication safely is also important. Do not throw it in the trash or flush it down the toilet. Many pharmacies have take-back programs. They ensure that unused medication is disposed of safely.

Communicating with your doctor and pharmacist is key. Inform them about all the medications you are taking. This includes over-the-counter drugs and supplements. They can check for any possible interactions. Keep a list of your medications with you. This can be helpful in emergencies. If you miss a dose, follow the instructions on what to do. Never double the dose to make up for a missed one. Safe medication practices ensure effective treatment.

Comprehension Questions:

1. Why is it important to follow the doctor's instructions for medication?

____

2. What can help you keep track of your medication?

____

3. Why should you read the medication label?

____

4. How should medication be stored?

____

5. What should you do with expired medication?

____

6. Why is it important to inform your doctor about all the medications you are taking?

____

7. Summarize each paragraph in your own words.

____

Exercise 10- Read the text aloud before answering the questions.

Developing Healthy Habits

Healthy habits are essential for a long and fulfilling life. Eating a balanced diet provides necessary nutrients. Include fruits, vegetables, whole grains, and lean proteins in your meals. Avoid processed foods and sugary drinks. Drinking plenty of water is important for hydration. Regular exercise keeps your body fit and strong. Aim for at least 30 minutes of physical activity daily. This can include walking, jogging, or yoga. Sleep is also crucial for good health. Aim for 7-9 hours of sleep each night.

Taking care of your mental and emotional health is crucial for overall well-being. Practice relaxation techniques like deep breathing and meditation to manage stress. Spend time with family and friends to improve your mood. Hobbies can also be a great way to relax. Avoid smoking and limit alcohol consumption. These habits can have negative effects on your health. Regular check-ups with your doctor are important. They help detect any health issues early. Following your doctor's advice ensures better health management.

Setting realistic goals can help you maintain healthy habits. Start with small, achievable changes. Gradually increase your efforts as you progress. Keeping a journal can track your habits and progress. Celebrate your achievements, no matter how small. Staying motivated is key to maintaining healthy habits. Joining a support group can provide encouragement. Remember that developing healthy habits takes time. Be patient and persistent for long-term success.

Comprehension Questions:

1. What should a balanced diet include?

____

2. How much physical activity is recommended daily?

____

3. How many hours of sleep should one have each night?

____

4. What are some techniques for managing stress?

____

5. What habits are advised to avoid or limit?

____

6. Why should someone keep a journal?

____

7. Summarize each paragraph in your own words.

____

Exercise 11- Read the text aloud before answering the questions.

Navigating College and Student Loans

Attending college can be a rewarding experience. It provides opportunities for learning and career growth. Choosing the right college is important. Consider factors like location, programs offered, and cost. Applying for financial aid can help manage college expenses. Scholarships, grants, and loans are common forms of aid. Researching and applying for scholarships can reduce the need for loans. It's important to understand the terms of student loans. This includes interest rates and repayment plans.

Managing student loans requires careful planning. Borrow only what you need to cover tuition and expenses. Create a budget to track your spending. This helps avoid unnecessary debt. Repayment of student loans begins after graduation. Understand your repayment options. Federal loans offer various repayment plans. These can include income-driven repayment. Private loans may have different terms. It's important to communicate with your loan servicer. They can provide information and assistance.

Staying on top of your student loans is important. Keep track of your loan balance and interest rates. Making payments on time helps avoid penalties. Setting up automatic payments can ensure you don't miss a due date. If you face financial difficulties, contact your loan servicer. They may offer deferment or forbearance options. Staying informed about loan forgiveness programs is beneficial. Some careers offer loan forgiveness after a certain period. Managing student loans responsibly ensures financial stability.

Comprehension Questions:

1. What should you consider when choosing a college?

____

2. What are some common forms of financial aid?

____

3. Why is it important to research and apply for scholarships?

____

4. How can creating a budget help manage student loans?

____

5. What is a repayment option for federal loans?

____

6. How can you ensure you don't miss the due date for payments?

____

7. Summarize each paragraph in your own words.

____

Understanding Housing and Rent

Finding a place to live is a significant decision. Consider factors like location, cost, and amenities. Amenities are the extra features or services you get with a property. These can be basic services like parking and laundry facilities or luxury options like a swimming pool and gym.

Renting is a common option for many people. Budgeting for rent and utilities is essential. Make sure your rent does not exceed 30% of your income. This helps to ensure you can afford other expenses. Setting up automatic payments can help avoid late fees. It's important to understand the terms of your lease. It outlines your responsibilities and rights as a tenant. It includes details on the monthly rent, security deposit, and lease duration. You should know the rules about maintenance and repairs. Landlords must provide a safe and habitable living environment. If there are issues, report them to your landlord immediately. Keep a record of all communications.

Understanding the process of moving out is also important. Give proper notice according to your lease terms. Clean the apartment thoroughly before leaving. This helps ensure you get your security deposit back. Returning the keys on time is essential. Consider your options if you plan to move to a new place. Research the new location and housing market. Finding a reliable moving company can make the process easier. Understanding housing and rent helps ensure a smooth living experience.

Comprehension Questions:

1. What should you consider when looking for a place to live?

____

2. Why is it important to read the lease agreement carefully?

____

3. How can budgeting help with rent and utilities?

____

4. What must landlords provide to tenants?

____

5. Why is it important to give proper notice before moving out?

____

6. How can understanding housing and rent help you?

____

7. Summarize each paragraph in your own words.

____

Exploring Trade Schools and Career Education

Trade schools offer specialized training for specific careers. Programs can include healthcare, technology, and skilled trades. These schools often have shorter programs than traditional colleges and teach practical skills needed for specific jobs. Understanding the different programs offered is important. Researching job prospects can help you choose the right program. Trade schools often have strong connections with employers. This can lead to quicker job placement opportunities after graduation.

Career and technical education (CTE) classes are also valuable. They provide hands-on learning experiences. These classes are available in high schools and community colleges. They cover various fields like business, engineering, and culinary arts. CTE programs help students gain practical skills. This makes them more competitive in the job market. Understanding the requirements for these programs is crucial. Some may have prerequisites or specific entry criteria.

Financing your education is an important consideration. Trade schools and CTE programs can be more affordable than traditional colleges. Financial aid options are available. This includes scholarships, grants, and loans. Researching and applying for financial aid can help manage costs. Balancing work and school can be challenging. Time management skills are essential. Staying focused and motivated is key to success. Understanding the benefits of trade schools and CTE classes can help you achieve your career goals.

Comprehension Questions:

1. What do trade schools offer?

____

2. How are trade schools different from traditional colleges?

____

3. What is the benefit of CTE classes?

____

4. Why is understanding program requirements important?

____

5. How can financial aid help with education costs?

____

6. Why are time management skills important in trade schools and CTE programs?

____

7. Summarize each paragraph in your own words.

____

Answer Keys for Reading Exercises

Exercise 1- Ensuring Safety in the Workplace

1. Workplace safety is important for protecting employees.
2. Employees should wear helmets, gloves, and safety glasses in hazardous environments.
3. Regular maintenance of equipment helps prevent accidents.
4. Supervisors conduct regular safety inspections to identify potential hazards early.
5. Keeping walkways clear of obstructions helps prevent slips and trips.
6. Employees should be able to use fire extinguishers and first aid kits.

7. - Federal income taxes require correct filing by individuals and businesses.
    - Sales taxes vary by location and fund local services.
    - Effective tax management, including budgeting, seeking professional advice, and staying informed about changes, is crucial for financial stability.

Exercise 8- Navigating Health Care Services and Insurance

1. Health care services include visits to doctors, hospitals, and clinics.
2. Preventive care helps in the early detection of health issues.

7. - Workplace safety is vital, requiring awareness of safety procedures and the use of protective gear.
   - Implementing safety measures is a shared responsibility and includes regular inspections and safety signs.
   - Emergency preparedness involves knowing how to respond to different emergencies, using safety tools, and participating in regular drills.

Exercise 2- The Importance of Effective Communication

1. Effective communication ensures everyone understands their roles and responsibilities.
2. Active listening involves paying attention to the speaker and responding appropriately.
3. Visual aids help make complex information easier to understand.
4. Barriers to communication include language differences, noise, and technical jargon.
5. Instant messaging can be used for quick communication.
6. Face-to-face communication builds stronger relationships.
7. - Effective communication involves active listening, polite language, and clear written communication.
   - Communication barriers can be overcome by making language simple and using visual aids.
   - It is important to try different communication methods to keep improving communication.

Exercise 3- Managing Your Household Budget

3. Health insurance helps cover the cost of medical expenses.
4. Co-pays are fixed amounts you pay for a service, and deductibles are amounts you pay before insurance covers the rest.
5. Keeping track of medical bills helps ensure accurate charges.
6. Having a primary care doctor helps manage your health and provides regular check-ups.
7. - Healthcare services, including preventive care, are vital for health.
   - Health insurance covers medical costs and requires understanding of co-pays, deductibles, and coverage details.
   - Access to healthcare varies by location, so it is important to stay informed about the services available and the health laws.

Exercise 9- Safely Using Medication

1. Following the doctor's instructions ensures proper treatment.
2. A pill organizer can help keep track of medication.
3. The medication label provides important instructions.
4. Medication should be stored in a cool, dry place away from children.
5. Expired medication should be disposed of safely through take-back programs.
6. Informing your doctor about all medications helps them check for interactions.
7. - Take medication exactly as prescribed, following dosage and instructions carefully.

1. Managing a household budget is important for financial stability.
2. Needs are essential expenses, while wants are optional.
3. Budgeting apps can help people stay organized and track spending.
4. A key strategy for responsibly using credit cards is to charge only what you can afford to pay off each month.
5. Emergency funds can cover unexpected events.
6. A financial advisor can provide personalized recommendations for managing finances.
7. - Managing a household budget is key to financial stability and involves tracking income, expenses, and setting financial goals.
   - Credit cards can be useful but must be managed responsibly to avoid debt and protect your credit score.
   - Building an emergency fund is crucial for financial security.

Exercise 4- Understanding US Elections

1. The first step in the election process is the nomination of candidates.
2. Debates are held to discuss important issues.
3. People can vote in person at polling stations, use mail-in ballots, or early voting options.
4. Voter registration ensures eligibility to vote.
5. The outcome of an election impacts laws, policies, and public services.
6. It is important for citizens to participate in elections as a way to express their opinions and fulfill their civic duty.

- Store medication properly, check expiration dates and safely dispose medication.
- Communicate with your doctor and pharmacist about all medications you are taking.

Exercise 10- Developing Healthy Habits

1. A balanced diet includes fruits, vegetables, whole grains, and lean proteins.
2. At least 30 minutes of physical activity is recommended daily.
3. One should have 7-9 hours of sleep each night.
4. Techniques for managing stress include deep breathing and meditation.
5. Smoking should be avoided and alcohol consumption should be limited.
6. A journal can help someone track their habits and progress.
7. - Healthy habits like having a balanced diet, regularly exercising and getting enough sleep are vital for a fulfilling life.
   - Managing stress, avoiding harmful habits, and regular medical check-ups are crucial for mental and emotional well-being.
   - Setting realistic goals, tracking progress, and staying motivated are key to maintaining healthy habits over time.

Exercise 11- Navigating College and Student Loans

1. Consider location, programs offered, and cost when choosing a college.

7. - Elections allow citizens to vote for their leaders after candidates are nominated and campaigns are conducted.
- Voting can be done in person, by mail, or through early voting.
- Elected leaders make decisions on laws and policies, so voter participation is vital at all levels of government.

Exercise 5- Civic Responsibilities in the United States

1. Obeying the law ensures order and safety.
2. Taxes fund public services like schools and roads.
3. Serving on a jury helps ensure a fair legal system.
4. Staying informed about political issues helps make educated voting decisions.
5. Volunteering and attending local meetings are two activities people can participate in.
6. Respecting the environment includes recycling and conserving resources.
7. - Obeying the law is important for maintaining order and safety.
- Voting, paying taxes, and serving on a jury are fundamental civic duties.
- Respecting the environment, participating in community activities, and helping others are vital for creating a strong society.

Exercise 6- Job Search and Interview Preparation

1. Your resume should highlight your skills and experience.
2. Networking can lead to job opportunities.

2. Scholarships, grants, and loans are common forms of financial aid.
3. Researching and applying for scholarships can reduce the need for loans.
4. Creating a budget helps track spending and avoid unnecessary debt.
5. Federal loans offer income-driven repayment.
6. Setting up automatic payments can ensure you don't miss a due date.
7. - Choosing the right college and understanding financial aid are important when attending college.
- Careful planning and budgeting are key to managing student loans.
- Staying informed about loans ensures long-term financial stability.

Exercise 12- Understanding Housing and Rent

1. Consider location, cost, and amenities when looking for a place to live.
2. Reading the lease agreement ensures you understand your responsibilities and rights.
3. Budgeting helps you afford rent, utilities, and other expenses.
4. Landlords must provide safe and habitable living environments.
5. Proper notice must be given so you can get your security deposit back.
6. Understanding housing and rent helps ensure a smooth living experience.
7. - Consider location, cost, and amenities, when finding a place to live.

3. Researching the company shows the employer that you are interested in the role.
4. Creating a positive first impression includes dressing appropriately and arriving on time.
5. Following up with a thank-you note shows appreciation for the opportunity and keeps you in the employer's mind.
6. Reflecting on your interview performance helps identify areas for improvement.
7. - Create a strong resume and network when job searching.
   - Preparing for an interview involves researching the company, practicing questions, dressing appropriately and arriving on time.
   - Follow up with a thank-you note, reflect on your performance, and stay persistent to after an interview.

Exercise 7- Understanding Federal Income and Sales Taxes

1. Federal income taxes are used for government revenue.
2. The amount of federal income tax is determined by your income.
3. Deductions and credits can include education expenses and charitable donations.
4. Retailers are responsible for collecting sales tax.
5. Sales taxes fund local services like schools and public safety.
6. Keeping records of your purchases helps ensure sales taxes are paid correctly.

- Renting involves budgeting, understanding your lease, and reporting issues to your landlord.
- When moving out, provide proper notice, clean the apartment, return the keys on time, and research new locations and moving options.

Exercise 13- Exploring Trade Schools and Career Education

1. Trade schools offer specialized training for specific careers.
2. Trade schools often have shorter programs than traditional colleges and teach practical skills.
3. CTE classes provide hands-on learning experiences.
4. Understanding program requirements ensures you meet the entry criteria.
5. Financial aid options help manage education costs.
6. Time management skills are important for balancing work and school.
7. - Trade schools provide specialized, shorter programs for specific careers and have strong job placement connections.
   - Career and technical education (CTE) classes offer hands-on learning in various fields.
   - Financing education through trade schools or CTE programs can be more affordable with financial aid and requires good time management and motivation.

Let's reflect on your progress.

1. What sounds did you review and practice?

2. What reading skills did you practice?

3. What strategies can you use to improve your reading comprehension skills?

4. What do you want your instructor to know about your challenges?

STRATEGIES TO INCREASE YOUR VOCABULARY AND IMPROVE

YOUR READING SKILLS

Strategies for Developing Reading Comprehension Skills

Reading Skills	Strategies
1. Decoding	o Break words into smaller parts. o Use phonics exercises to practice sounding out words. o Practice with flashcards and reading simple texts.
2. Vocabulary Building	o Learn one new word every day. o Use a dictionary to check and understand word meanings. o Create a list of new words and use them in sentences.

3. Fluency	o Read aloud daily.
	o Start with easy texts and gradually move to harder ones.
	o Record yourself reading to track your progress.
4. Comprehension	o After reading, write a summary of the main points. Write down the main ideas and details.
	o Answer questions about the text.
	o Discuss what you read with a friend or classmate.
5. Critical Thinking	o Think about why the author wrote the text.
	o Ask yourself questions about the characters and events.
	o Discuss your thoughts with others to gain different perspectives.
6. Inference	o Look for hints and clues in the text.
	o Try to predict what will happen next.
	o Confirm your predictions by continuing to read.
7. Retention	o Take notes while you read.
	o Highlight important information.
	o Review your notes regularly to reinforce learning.

Strategies to Increase Your Vocabulary

Strategies	Description
1. Read Regularly	o Read a variety of materials such as books, articles, and newspapers. o This helps you encounter new words in different contexts.
2. Use a Dictionary	o Look up new words in a dictionary. o Learn the meaning, pronunciation, and usage of the word.
3. Make Word Lists	o Keep a notebook or a digital list of new words. o Review the list daily to reinforce your learning.
4. Use Flashcards	o Create flashcards with new words and their definitions on the back. o Review the flashcards regularly to test your memory.
5. Practice Writing	o Write sentences or short paragraphs using new words. o This helps you understand how to use the words correctly.
6. Engage in Conversations	o Use new words in your daily conversations. o This reinforces your learning and helps you remember the words better.
7. Play Word Games	o Play games like Scrabble or word search puzzles. o These games make learning new words fun and interactive.

Important Strategies and Questions to Use When Reading Text

Strategies	Questions to Ask

1. Preview the Text	o Strategy: Look at the title, headings, and any pictures or graphs.
	o Questions to Ask:
	  1. What do the title and headings tell me about the text?
	  2. What do I think this text will be about?

2. Skim for Main Ideas	o Strategy: Read the first and last sentences of each paragraph.
	o Questions to Ask:
	  1. What are the main ideas in each paragraph?
	  2. Which sentences give the most important information?

3. Highlight Key Points	o Strategy: Use a highlighter or underline important sentences.
	o Questions to Ask:
	  1. What information seems most important?
	  2. Which parts of the text should I remember?

4. Summarize	o Strategy: Write a brief summary of what you read.
	o Questions to Ask:
	  1. What is the text mainly about?
	  2. Can I explain the main points in my own words?

5. Ask Questions	o Strategy: Think of questions about the text as you read.
	o Questions to Ask:
	  1. What do I want to know more about?
	  2. What questions do I have about the topic?

6. Make Connections	o Strategy: Relate the text to your own experiences or other things you've read.
	o Questions to Ask:
	  1. How does this text relate to what I already know?
	  2. Can I think of a similar experience or another text on this topic?

7. Reflect and Review	o Strategy: Take time to think about what you have read after you finish.
	o Questions to Ask:
	  1. What have I learned from this text?
	  2. How can I use this information in the future?

Make use of all the strategies you read about in this book. Review and practice them every week until you master them. Good luck with your learning journey!

Coaching for Better Learning (CBL) helps adult education and workforce service providers improve and create professional development and instructional systems to maximize student engagement, retention—and learning.

CBL takes pride in publishing learner-centered student textbooks designed to prepare learners for standardized assessments (CASAS, TABE 11&12, HiSET, and GED) and to assist instructors in covering course curricula and standards— aligned with NRS, ELPS, and WIOA expectations—with confidence.

Our publications also include teaching guides, test prep tools, and study guides that foster reflective learning, ensuring sustained engagement in active learning. Find our meticulously crafted textbooks on our book page (cbledu.com) or major platforms—like Amazon, Barnes & Noble, and Ingram Spark.

CBL also guides adult education and workforce programs in establishing robust professional development programs—training, peer-mentoring, coaching, community of practices (CoPs), and instructional systems—fostering a culture of continuous improvement and contributing to higher learner retention and success rates.

Additionally, we offer workshops and PD sessions for adult educators and classroom instructors. We design and implement our sessions using robust and evidence-based frameworks (Bloom Taxonomy, brain-based learning, systems thinking) and adult learning theories (Transformational Learning, Andragogy, Theory of Margin, and Self-Directed learning).

Our diverse solutions are intricately designed to enrich students' learning experiences and simplify instructors' jobs. Examples of our professional development solutions include:

1. High-impact teaching practices.
2. Promoting high-impact student retention practices.
3. Giving clear and effective instructions.
4. Digital literacy that focuses on learning.
5. Reflective teaching practices to maximize learning.
6. Learning theories and frameworks for high-impact instructions.
7. Leveraging instructional technology (TPACK: Technological, Pedagogical, and Content Knowledge) for high-impact teaching.
8. Applying evidence-based strategies for engaging learners and maximizing their performance on standardized testing.

If you have questions about instructional systems, textbooks, or student learning and retention, contact us today at teamcbl@cbledu.com or 410-960-4082.

MORE TEXTBOOKS BY CBL

ADULT ED
MATH
NUMBER SYSTEM, NUMBER SENSE, AND OPERATIONS PREPARING
FOR
CASAS, TABE 11 & 12, HISET, AND GED TESTING
BY COACHING FOR BETTER LEARNING

ADULT ED
MATH
GEOMETRY PREPARING
FOR
CASAS, TABE 11 & 12, HISET, AND GED TESTING
BY COACHING FOR BETTER LEARNING

CBL COACHING
FOR BETTER LEARNING
Math
Practice Worksheets and Workbook for Adult Students
A learner-centered tool designed to help students practice and master the four operations while preparing them for CASAS Math GOALS 2, TABE 11 and 12, ACT, HISET, GED tests, and IET programs.

SKILLS FOR SUCCESS IN CAREER AND TECHNICAL EDUCATION (CTE)
STUDENT GUIDE
A SYSTEMATIC WAY TO MASTER ORGANIZATIONAL AND SOFT SKILLS
CBL COACHING
FOR BETTER LEARNING
BY COACHING FOR BETTER LEARNING, LLC

HOW TO ACHIEVE BETTER STUDENT RETENTION IN ADULT EDUCATION
Secrets to becoming an indispensable adult-ed teacher that provides a learning experience that's hard to walk away from (and keeps administrators happy!)
TEDDY EDOUARD

TABE 11 & 12
CONSUMABLE
STUDENT READING
MANUAL
FOR LEVEL E
Preparing Adult Learners for TABE 11 & 12 Reading Tests and for Vocational Training and College Entrance Reading Exams
By Coaching for Better Learning, LLC

TABE 11 & 12
CONSUMABLE
STUDENT READING
MANUAL
FOR LEVEL M
Preparing Adult Learners for TABE 11 & 12 Reading Tests and for Vocational Training and College Entrance Reading Exams
By Coaching for Better Learning, LLC

TABE 11 & 12
CONSUMABLE
STUDENT READING
MANUAL
FOR LEVEL D
Preparing Adult Learners for TABE 11 & 12 Reading Tests and for Vocational Training and College Entrance Reading Exams
By Coaching for Better Learning, LLC

TABE 11 & 12
STUDENT
LANGUAGE
MANUAL
FOR LEVEL E
Preparing Adult Learners for TABE 11 & 12 Language Tests and for Vocational Training and College Entrance Exams
By Coaching for Better Learning, LLC

TABE 11 & 12
STUDENT
LANGUAGE
MANUAL
FOR LEVEL M
Preparing Adult Learners for TABE 11 & 12 Language Tests and for Vocational Training and College Entrance Exams
By Coaching for Better Learning, LLC

Preparing Adult Learners for TABE 11 & 12 Math Tests and for Vocational Training Entrance Math Exams
TABE 11 & 12
Consumable
Student Math
Workbook
FOR LEVEL E
By Coaching for Better Learning, LLC

Preparing Adult Learners for TABE 11 & 12 Math Tests and for Vocational Training Entrance Math Exams
TABE 11 & 12
Consumable
Student Math
Workbook
FOR LEVEL M
By Coaching for Better Learning, LLC

Preparing Adult Learners for TABE 11 & 12 Math Tests and for Vocational Training Entrance Math Exams
TABE 11 & 12
Consumable
Student Math
Workbook
FOR LEVEL D
By Coaching for Better Learning, LLC

Preparing Adult Learners for TABE 11 & 12 Math Tests and for Vocational Training Entrance Math Exams
TABE 11 & 12
Consumable
Student Math
Workbook
FOR LEVEL A
By Coaching for Better Learning, LLC

CBL COACHING
FOR BETTER LEARNING
Workbook
Number and Letter Tracing for Adult Students
This tool is designed to help adult students practice and master handwriting. It is appropriate for literacy, ESL, and ABE classes.

READING NOTEBOOK & JOURNAL
For Adult Students
By Coaching For Better Learning
CBL COACHING

MATH NOTEBOOK & JOURNAL
For Adult Students
By Coaching For Better Learning
CBL COACHING

BOOK 1
PHONICS AND LIFE SKILLS READING
FOR
Adult Literacy, ABE, and ESL Students
Turning Learners into Proficient Readers
CBL COACHING
FOR BETTER LEARNING

BOOK 2
PHONICS AND LIFE SKILLS READING
FOR
Adult Literacy, ABE, and ESL Students
Turning Learners into Proficient Readers
CBL COACHING
FOR BETTER LEARNING